Beyond Words
South African Poetics

an apples & snakes project

Beyond Words

defeye series (No. 3)
Printed and Bound in the United Kingdom

Published by flipped eye publishing, 2009
under the defeye series
www.flippedeye.net
All Rights Reserved

First Edition
Copyright © individual authors 2009

This title is the text to the touring production, *Beyond Words*:
produced by apples & snakes.

Cover Layout © Petraski, 2009
Series Design © flipped eye publishing, 2009

ISBN-10: 1-905233-26-4
ISBN-13: 978-1-905233-26-7

Text laid out using BaskervilleMT.

LOTTERY FUNDED

Beyond Words

Foreword

Poetry is life distilled – Gwendolyn Brooks

Beyond Words is about connections and about open-ended possibilities, about the refusal of poetry to accept any limitations as to where it may venture. *Beyond Words* celebrates the indomitable and irrepressible spirit of human utterance.

Distilled in this collection of new work is the vibrant historical lifeblood of South Africa. The arc of time bridged by the births and maturings of the four poets showcased here takes in a world war, the scandalous apartheid system of racial segregation, decades of oppression and of protest, of bannings and detentions, of tragedy, of heroism, the dismantling of discriminatory legislation, the freeing of Nelson Mandela, the stages of negotiation, democracy, reconciliation, transition, inexorable change.

These poets represent generations that have both experienced directly and been indelibly influenced by this momentous history. Yet their concerns, references and aspirations resonate far beyond the borders of the country that defines them, and the continent that encompasses that nation, demonstrating a range as varied as their personal stories.

Keorapetse William Kgositsile (Bra Willie) is South Africa's national poet laureate, who lived in exile from 1961 and, particularly during the 1970s in the USA made interactive links with pan-African creativity. Uncompromisingly outspoken as a performance artist, and encouraging of those who have come later, he is ideally placed to muse:

> Poem, I know you are reluctant to sing
> when there is no joy in your heart,
> but I have wondered all these years
> why you did not or could not give
> answer when Langston Hughes, who
> wondered as he wandered, asked:
> what happens to a dream deferred?

His visionary poem *No Boundaries* gives a qualified lead that is as much a warning:

> With informed hope
> and resolve we must know
> how to move forward to a landscape
> where our dreams cannot be turned into nightmare,
> where our dreams are always in sight,
> where we must again
> redden the blackest folds
> of our memory and intent.

Don Mattera - like Kgositsile a survivor of the apartheid years, and a founding member of the Black Consciousness movement – writes affectingly and with tenderness about what "those who marched" now pass on to their offspring. Acknowledging that "Perhaps it was a weakness on our part / that we did not hate enough / or that we loved too much", he expresses an optimism tinged with disappointment:

> And children again came
> pure and clean
> dressed in love's sweet fire
> bringing New Seeds
> and where a despairing people stood,
> the children planted a New Africa
> For a new world (*Child*)

The conclusion he delivers is ultimately hopeful:

> bring back the glorious grain
> for the coming victory of 'This Child'
> and heal our seething sombre souls
> that we might lift one another and,
> live again. . . (*Song for 'This Child'*)

The legacy of their elders' struggles and activism is used well by the younger two poets, two women, the counsel heeded.

In the poetry of Phillippa Yaa de Villers, seasoned by her theatrical training, compassion vies with sharp-eyed outrage. She can be as combative in her language as her namesake the legendary warrior queen Yaa Asantewaa, but her work makes nuanced and precise observations even as it deals with the way things should be in an ideal world. Her poignant *What the Dead Say* conjures an image of modern urban Africa as a bevy of haunted, world-weary young women "with that lewd, innocent look around the eyes / That girls get when they've been used too soon". Meanwhile:

> the dead walk the streets,
> their last cries woven into the bricks of its fortresses:
> "We have no place in this history that they say
> is ours. Who are these heroes? Strangers stare out of books
> like products in foreign shop windows. Please,
> please, show me a picture of me.
> Tell my story."

Lebogang Mashile, a versatile practitioner in many creative fields, is conscious that the consequences of political oppression are painfully felt in the personal context, "Where is the love when there is no respect?" she asks. *God blues for Mama* depicts a long-suffering woman who "takes pain as the price for a life that has always been the same", *Green Hands* is about a father who takes out his frustrations – "at work he's a boy / At home he's a man" – by hitting "his" woman.

> My father has no word for love
> So his hands plant them (*Green Hands*)

Mashile's poem *I Dance to Know Who I Am* expresses things that lie beyond words. "My body speaks a wordless language," she writes. Her imagery unifies the corporeal and the spiritual: "The fabric of my flesh is threaded with songs (…) My body is a text in constant communication…."

The elusiveness of language as well as its significant absences exercises and provokes all the poets. As Bra Willie notes:

> In my language there is no word for *citizen*… That word came to us as part of the package that contained the bible and the rifle. But *moagi*, resident, is there and it has nothing to do with any border or boundary you may or may not have crossed before waking up on the piece of earth where you currently live. (*No Serenity Here*)

These activist poets are residents of the world, elucidating its contradictions and conundrums, while ensuring that "the tapestry of memory", as Kgositsile has it, engages the present "with informed hope and resolve".

Beyond Words is an unfinished conversation with the future.

Margaret Busby, October 2009

List of Poets

Keorapetse Kgositsile   11

Phillippa Yaa de Villiers   19

Don Mattera   28

Lebo Mashile   37

Biographies   47

Keorapetse Kgositsile

No Boundaries

I possess neither wings
nor the magician's mischief
but, believe me, I can fly;
and I can also be a landscape
of mirrors that name whatever moves
or has pretensions to be alive.

On the wingspan of my desire,
easy as the approach of any day,
you can clearly remember
I can fly to any place
or moment fertile with memory
or create fresh ones without a single boundary
though our lives remain so pathetically prosaic.

With informed hope
and resolve we must know
how to move forward to a landscape
where our dreams cannot be turned into nightmare,
where our dreams are always in sight,
where we must again
redden the blackest folds
of our memory and intent.

No Serenity Here

An omelette cannot be unscrambled. Not even the one prepared in the crucible of 19th-century sordid European design.

When Europe cut up this continent into little pockets of its imperialist want and greed it was not for aesthetic reasons, nor was it in the service of any African interest, intent, or purpose.

When, then, did the brutality of imperialist appetite and aggression evolve into something of such ominous value to us that we torture, mutilate, butcher in ways hideous beyond the imagination, rape women, men, even children and infants for having woken up on what we now claim, with perverse possessiveness and territorial chauvinism, to be our side of the boundary that until only yesterday arrogantly defined where a piece of one European property ended and another began? In my language there is no word for *citizen*, which is an ingredient of that 19th-century omelette. That word came to us

as part of the package that contained the bible and the rifle.
But *moagi*, resident, is there and it has nothing to do with any
border or boundary you may or may not have crossed before
waking up on the piece of earth where you currently live.

Poem, I know you are reluctant to sing
when there is no joy in your heart,
but I have wondered all these years
why you did not or could not give
answer when Langston Hughes, who
wondered as he wandered, asked:
what happens to a dream deferred?

I wonder now
why we are somewhere we did not aim
to be. Like my sister
who could report from any
place where people live,
I fear the end of peace
and I wonder if
that is perhaps why
our memories of struggle
refuse to be erased,
our memories of struggle
refuse to die

we are not strangers
to the end of peace,
we have known women widowed
without any corpses of husbands
because the road to the mines,
like the road to any war,
is long and littered with casualties – even
those who still walk and talk

when Nathalie, whose young eyes know things, says:
there is nothing left after wars, only other wars
wake up whether you are witness or executioner -
the victim, whose humanity you can never erase,
knows with clarity more solid than granite
that no matter which side you are on,
any day or night, an injury to one
remains an injury to all

somewhere on this continent
the voice of the ancients warns
that those who shit on the road
will meet flies on their way back,
so perhaps you should shudder under the weight
of nightmares when you consider what
thoughts might enter the hearts of our neighbours,

what frightened or frightening memories might jump up
when they hear a South African accent

even the sun, embarrassed, withdraws her warmth
from this atrocious defiance and unbridled denial
of the ties that should bind us here and always
and the night will not own any of this stench
of betrayal which has desecrated our national anthem,
so do not tell me of NEPAD or AU,
do not tell me of SADC
and please do not try to say shit about
ubuntu or any other such neurosis of history

again I say, while I still have voice,
remember, always
remember that you are what you do,
past any saying of it

our memories of struggle
refuse to be erased
our memories of struggle
refuse to die.

My mothers, fathers of my father and me,
how shall I sing to celebrate life
when every space in my heart is surrounded by corpses?
Whose thousand thundering voices shall I borrow to shout
once more: *Daar is kak in die land!*?

Letter from Havana
(for Baby K)

A while back I said
with my little hand upon
the tapestry of memory and my loin
leaning on the blues to find voice:
If loving you is wrong
I do not want to do right

Now though I do not possess
a thousand thundering voices
like Mazisi kaMdabuli weKunene
nor Chris Abani's mischievous courage
as I trace the shape of desire and longing,
I wish I was a cartographer of dreams,
but what I end up with is this stubborn question:
Should I love my heart more
because every time I miss you
that is where I find you?

Phillippa Yaa de Villiers

What the Dead Say

Cities stand
    like ravished women
called Maputo, Accra, Mombasa;
      on a beach
of bleached memory;
      they are torn, shattered, only half-decent,
with that lewd, innocent look around their eyes
    that girls get when they've been used too soon:
they know how to please and how to get
    what they need. They watch sailors come
and go. The waves blow their minds
    back to the first sharp pain as
hard men forced themselves into their house of dreams
    and buildings bled history
into the soil of time. Now, a tattered cover girl
    seduces visitors to exotic destinations while
the dead walk the streets,

       their last cries woven into the bricks of its fortresses:
"We have no place in this history that they say
    is ours. Who are these heroes?
Strangers stare out of books
   like products in foreign shop windows. Please,
             please, show me a picture of me.
  Tell my story."

Eating for Two

Hunger grumbles,
fragrant food seduces,
the stomach
rumbles;
genteel lips conceal gushing saliva,
our eyes journey to the Sunday chicken,
we look away to pray,
amen gives way
to flashing knives and mashing teeth:
for now, hunger retreats.

The tourist asks
why Africa is hungry.
Divided the heart:
we don't know how to answer.

Outside
hunger humbles,
a beggar reaches into
the cold skies of a stranger's eyes
as hunger tumbles
hope
into a gutter of stuttering
half-baked dreams
and aborted fantasies
and bungles plans
and scrambles opportunities,
and hunger stumbles
along blocked synapses,
bumps its head repeatedly as
bulimic greed
dry heaves
its simulated grief,
stuffing images of lust
into a seething cavity
of need.

The tourist asks
how we plan
to solve the problem.
Subtracted the stomach:

we don't know how to answer.

Hard-working
hunger, the farmer
sows rows of skeletons,
and waits for an empty harvest.
Hunger builds a boat of bones,
casts a net of starving eyes,
people drown in dust without resisting.
There is no second course;
dying fragments loaf
along the desert's shore.

The tourist is the authority.
They know how to stay alive! We are still learning.
Politely we wipe our mouths and give thanks for what we have
received: pronunciation and chicken on Sundays.
Contradiction multiplied:
we don't know how to answer.

We live by killing,
we can't explain.
Perhaps hunger will come to our table one day.

But by then,
most probably,
the tourist will have
gone away.

Anthem: the possibility of evolution or the evolution of possibility

Words sketch images on the air.
Voice sets them on fire. I am
mostly water.

I watch traditions foot stamping,
dancing themselves   back to divinity
and a heavy flood
bursts between the chambers of my heart
                                        bright red
vital

I am alive:
my heart the same size as this fist and I,
as little as this finger. We are all connected,
the living and the dead.
We arrive in life and then it
walks away from us;

leaving our bones behind
and our minds are as wide as the universe.

Human evolution began in this corner of the earth,
our ancestors left their dust as chromosomes
in each of us, they made a home,
and hominids stood up as humans and walked,
languages fell out of our mouths and talked, walked their way
into and out of landscapes, mindscapes. We walk in words,
creating as we need:
we stand   shadow-thin
and then
we chase the horizon   disappearing
until
we reappear again.

Miracles exist. Victims become heroes:
a man with no legs is the fastest runner in the world.
A woman who cannot walk swims to golden glory.
Our brains are two halves, reflecting duality,
a system of opposite pairs like an on-off switch:
black white right wrong man woman night day
Caster Semenya, the intersex athlete is
an invitation
to consider the end of two-way thinking. A provocation

to refine our definition of what it means to be human
or woman. A conundrum. We find ourselves in a hard land
that we don't understand, we've never been here before but
this is what the future looks like. We will stumble upon words
to tether our uniqueness to the soil.

Miracles exist, we carve them out of our bodies,
we hammer them out of stone and copper,
we weave them out of desire:
For what the world does not contain,
our minds create a home, we are making this world,
this world that has no borders because it does not exist,
until we take the time to make the world again.

We are alive,
our hearts as big as our fists and we
as little as our fingers. We are all connected,
the living and the dead, and our minds are infinite
as the universe.

Don Mattera

Child

The leaves of the tree of my life
grow brown and thin,
soon they will fall to earth
and be forgotten
Much fruit has withered,
only a few strong boughs remain
but they too will be broken
by the erosion of time.
But of all my fruit
of all things dear and close to my heart,
was you and the hope manifest
in your being -
you, the offspring of an invincible dream.
All my seeking my fervent cries
and the depth of longing
were but distant echoes,
my wounds mere relics.
Yet, all I asked of you

was that you remember me
for what I tried to do, tried to offer,
so that a New Bright Sun would rise
on your day;
that a portion of my dream
for the freedom of my people
would find a place in your song and in your dreams,
that my name and those who marched with me
would be recorded on your scroll
What do we live for
if not to be remembered by our beloved?

I wanted to offer you sonnets
and poems of springbuds unfurling
to the sunlight,
sing about the fir trees pointing at God,
but how could I sing of the tree
when beneath it, my people laid in fear
and their wounds unfurled the horror
of existence,
their prayers like cries of death
their hearts cursing God?
Yet amid all the hate and hostility
I did not hate those who held us in servitude
though I tried hard to
Perhaps it was weakness on our part

that we did not hate enough
or that we loved too much
yet, how much is too much?
It is a true though that revolutions
are born out of love;
love for land and liberty
love of humanity
and love of oneself.
I watched many suns sink,
saw phantom shadows raise their ominous banners
and heard my name called
while dreams, desires of a lifetime
whittled under violent feet,
I held the bloody scroll
with shaky, awe-struck hands,
the cup did not pass untouched
from these lips that hungered after justice.
How often did I ask God
if there was something we missed,
or a teaching that went unheeded
from the prophets in whose shadows
we walked?
But your blood was changing;
a vibrant light glowed in your eyes,
a sacred fire of unseen power within you

claimed its bounty of life,
all tomorrows belonged to you,
yours through the strength and defiance
that flowed in a struggle carved from God's image.
The world was teeming with unrest
everywhere men and women were fighting to be heard,
to walk upright in the land of their ancestors.
It was no different in our continent
nor in our country where the tingods
taught their offspring to despise and
humiliate us.
Yet there were many good, well-meaning,
justice-loving white folk,
men and women of conscience
who sacrificed their days that others
might be free.
Those who did not conform were broken;
those who refused to break
were imprisoned or killed,
others persecuted and driven to self-exile,
but many millions remained silent
enjoying the ill-gotten harvest.
I was not asking you to hate whites
for it would have negated my own humanity;
the anger and enmity I felt was for the denial

of human dignity
and the sacred right to love unhindered.
I tell you that even our finer emotions,
those which sustained us with inner succour
when debasement exacted
its toll on our lives,
were made into lies with which
we were deceived.
But as there were evil white people
so too were there black ones
who became the tools
with which we were fooled
and indoctrinated;
black men and women who crawled
for the colonial crumbs of comfort
and sold their souls for money
Child, I watched the slow decay
of our people in the cities
in the dry foodless reserves
in the prisons, and a thousand angry rivers
rushed through me:
their deaths were not in vain,
they were the foundation of our freedom
I looked at you and the fear I had
for death faltered,

when I touched your dimpled hands
drank your warm laughter
certain that you would outlive the tempest
that would lash the land
in order to set it free.
Those words I gave you
were testament of my deep love for you
and for our beloved land
written in the hope that you would remember
those valiant folk who marched with me
and in remembering, cherish the legacy
bequeathed to you through their blood
in the final hope that a New Bright Sun
would rise on your Tomorrow. . .
It was in a dream, by the river
I heard the plaintive cries
of a continent and a world in chains
still singing the ancient song of slavery:
how long, Lord, how long. . .
and the moon fell on shimmering water
lighting up the darkness
and their voices rose high
breaking the fetters that bound Africa
and our war-torn world.
And children again came

pure and clean
dressed in love's sweet fire
bringing New Seeds
and where a despairing people stood,
the children planted a New Africa
for a New World. . .

Song for 'This Child'

For 'This Child' of the world
Let 'This Child's' bright eyes
conquer the cold darkness
shine across the tortured earth
great pieces of crystal star
to silence the drums of war
flesh out the bones of hunger
heal the frightened hearts
Let the voice of bruised innocence
roll and cleanse every defiled hill
austere mountain and prostrate lea
the deep, bleeding gorge, pour and fill
with unfettered sounds of joy
the raging river, the writhing sea,
remove the masks of false pretence
'This Child' in a world befuddled,
may sunshine and sweet parenthood,

clear skies in the crimson East,
warm the fireplace of your dreams,
and fill your house with love
make gold the grain of childhood,
brown the bread for Tomorrow's feast
Fly on the wings of the wind
and soothe the plaintive pain
of a world in haste to die,
bring out the living seed again
and where we stand without dignity
and we fall and cry, come 'This Child'
and plant a New Humanity

Arise with yearning, searching eyes
and seek out the solemn darkness,
silence the cold voice of death,
bring back the glorious grain
for the coming victory of 'This Child'
and heal our seething sombre souls
that we might lift one another and,
live again. . .

Lebo Mashile

God Blues for Mama

God is always there, Mama said
After screams in the dark
Broken tears in the night
Bruises and fear

God never runs, Mama said
He died on a cross
Papa was cross
She bled from her head

God never hides, Mama said
She's at church every night
Close to him
The Lord lives inside

God always protects, Mama said
God is love – love is God

Where is love when there is no respect?

God always saves, Mama said
20 years is a gift from above
A gift she'd never exchange

God never forsakes, Mama said
She takes pain as the price for a life
that has always been the same

I dance to know who I am

I.

I dance to know who I am
When I am in motion
I move to find the rhythm
That permeates this commotion
This body is a pen
Its movements are words
Every dance is a tale
I write about this world
It is the physical expression of thoughts
Intertwined with flesh
Where melody and ligaments meet
Infused with breath and sweat
I dance to bring light into darkness
I move to understand what lives beneath the skin
I dance to trace the cord that leads
To who I truly am

II.

My body speaks a wordless language
Its movements are philosophy
There's logic to this living instrument
The dancer sculpting clay that breathes

My body speaks a magic language stripping my soul bare
So that the viewer might be seen
I give every part of myself to strangers
And they find themselves in my dreams

My body speaks a loving language
I travel the world through self-study
My voice is formed by limbs in motion
Wordless expression in a world
Where words are currency

Dance is the intimate exchange of information
With inspiration linking two souls through breath
Is the part of me you take home with you
The unknown you that has been revealed to yourself?
We rely on other bodies to make our bodies whole
The entire complete body is a landscape unknown
Dance can heal a body, can make the broken whole

Dance can never leave a body
It gives body to the soul
I dance with my whole self
I dance to make myself whole
I dance to know myself
Because the self is unknown

The fabric of my flesh is threaded with songs
It is embedded with rhythms as fluid as oceans
And just as long
My hearts percussion flows to my feet
As they play notes on the ground
At once linking past and present
Memory
Magic
Image
Soul and sound
We can read each others bodies
To reveal the fine print of energy
The cord that pulls the power of movement
Throughout our human superstring
Rituals in constant transformation
Create a cultural symphony
Life is moving to the soundtrack of time
Dance is an act of remembering

Humanity is a collective body divine
My dance is my offering

I could use a million words to say
What my body can with one move
My language is physical
Primal
Not primitive
The language I live and love
Is the language I choose
I am a dancer who thinks
A thinker who dances
Movements infused with the ideas in my mind
My body is designed to absorb information
I wouldn't trade my mind for an engineer's mind
My body is a text in constant communication
I wouldn't trade my mind for an executive's mind
Even though the lows are low
And the highs are high
Even though after the show
No one sees the loneliness inside

My body speaks a loving language
Channelling words from my pen
Flying high up above

Dance is an intimate exchange
An infinite connection
Dance is an act of love

Green Hands

He makes life grow
He kills the life in my mother
She knows how to hold blows
The green love grows inside her

He makes life grow
In suburban gardens where his hands feed us
At work he's a boy
At home he's a man
That's why he needs us

He makes life grow
This boy called my father
My father is a boy growing green with love
That's why he hits her

He makes life grow
This boy's heart is like a garden
My father has no words for love
So his hands plant them

Biographies

KEORAPETSE KGOSITSILE

Professor Keorapetse Kgositsile (Bra Willie) is South Africa's National Poet Laureate. In 1961 Kgositsile was one of the first young members of the African National Congress instructed to leave the country by the leadership of the national liberation movement.

He achieved fame as a poet during his years in exile in the United States in the 60s and 70s as a central figure among African-American poets, encouraging interest in Africa as well as the practice of poetry as a performance art, and his name was known in the New York City jazz clubs for his vibrant readings. He was one of the first to bridge the gap between African poetry and Black poetry in the United States.The Last Poets, who are credited for laying the groundwork for the emergence of hip-hop, took their name from a poem he wrote in the 60s.

Kgositsile is one of the most internationally acclaimed and widely published South African poets. His poetry collections include *My Name is Afrika, Heartprints, To the Bitter End, If I Could Sing, This Way I Salute You* and he has taught Literature and Creative Writing at a number of universities in the United States and on the African continent including, the University of Denver, University of California at Los Angeles and the universities of Dar es Salaam, Nairobi, Botswana, Zambia and Fort Hare.

He has been the recipient of a number of literary awards including, the Gwendolyn Brooks Poetry Prize, the Harlem Cultural Council Poetry Award, the Conrad Kent Rivers Memorial Poetry Award, the Herman Charles Bosman Prize and a number of others. In 2008 he was awarded the National Order of Ikhamanga Silver (OIS)

LEBO MASHILE

The poet, performer, actress, presenter and producer Lebogang Mashile, the daughter of exiled South Africans, was born in the U.S. in 1979. At the age of sixteen she and her parents returned to their home country. It was while she was studying law and international relations at Wits University in Johannesburg that the desire to work as an artist took hold of her.

In 2003 she co-founded the "Feel a Sistah!" Spoken Word Collective alongside Myesha Jenkins, Ntsiki Mazwai and Napo Masheane, which gained wide-spread popularity. Her lyrical and gutsy poems in the collection *A Ribbon of Rhythm* (2005) speak about life in the new South Africa and Mashile's self-produced album *Lebo Mashile Live!* combines her performance poetry with hip-hop, house and R&B. Her most recent work is a book of poems *Flying Above the Sky* (2008).

Lebo Mashile, has featured on numerous covers of South African entertainment and lifestyle magazines and was voted one of South Africa's Awesome Women of 2005 by Cosmopolitan Magazine. Named one of the Top 100 youth in South Africa by the Mail & Guardian in 2006 and 2007, she has also toured in Kenya, Austria, Germany, Cuba, Jamaica, Ireland, Zimbabwe, the United States, Britain, and Switzerland.

In 2006 she was awarded the prestigious Noma award. The Jury characterised her poetry as of "a distinct oral flavour, developing oral poetry and performance beyond the boundaries of the poetry of the era of resistance". She was also the recipient of the 2007 City Press/ Rapport Woman of Prestige Award. Mashile lives in Johannesburg.

DONATO FRANCISCO MATTERA

Donato Francisco Mattera has been celebrated as a journalist, editor, writer and poet. He is also acknowledged as one of the foremost activists in the struggle for a democratic South Africa, and helped found the Union of Black Journalists and the Congress of South African Writers.

Born in 1935 in the Western Native Township (now Westbury) across the road from Sophiatown, Mattera can lay claim to an intriguingly diverse lineage: his paternal grandfather was Italian, and he has Tswana, Khoi-Khoi and Xhosa blood in his veins. Yet diversity was hardly being celebrated at that time; in one of apartheids' most infamous actions, the vibrant multicultural area of Sophiatown was destroyed in 1955 and replaced with the white suburb of Triomf; the wrenching displacement can be felt in Mattera's writing.

Writing was certainly not an obvious conclusion to his youth, which had been characterized by gangs, violence and jail. Partly under the influence of Father Trevor Huddleston, Mattera began wielding a pen rather than a knife, yet with equal facility; using the struggle as his subject, he went on to produce a series of poems, stories and plays of force and originality. The authorities responded by raiding his house, imprisoning and torturing him, and banning him for ten years. It was during these tumultuous times that Mattera wrote the poems contained in *Azanian Love Song* (1983, 2007). His other publications are *The Five Magic Pebbles* (1992, 2007), *The Story Teller* (Short Stories, 1989), *Gone With the Twilight: Coming of Age in South Africa* (Autobiography, 1987), *Memory is the Weapon* (Autobiography, 2007).

Mattera serves as an active patron of several well-known charities in Johannesburg.

PHILLIPPA YAA de VILLIERS

Phillippa Yaa de Villiers was brought up in Halfway House near Johannesburg, she studied in Grahamstown and Paris and lived in Los Angeles before returning to settle in Johannesburg.

She studied theatre at the Lecoq School in Paris, and after a Journalism degree at Rhodes University, also obtained an Honours in Dramatic Art and Scriptwriting from the University of the Witwatersrand. de Villiers worked as a scriptwriter for television and radio for ten years, contributing to local series such as *Soul City, Soul Buddyz, Thetha Msawawa, Tsha Tsha, Takalani Sesame* and *Backstage*.

A widely published writer, she has represented South Africa in Sweden, at the International Festival of Poetry in Havana, Cuba, PassaPorta International Literary Festival in Belgium and Word Power in London. Her work is published in *The Edinburgh Review: Voices from Africa, Botsotso 14, Just Keep Breathing, We Are*, and *Poui*, the Cave Hill Journal of Poetry and Literature from Barbados; and her short story 'Keeping everything the same' was selected by JM Coetzee to be included in *New Writing from Africa* (Kingjames Books, 2009.) In 2005 she received the runner up Best Writer Award and the Audience Appreciation Award at the Pansa Festival of Contemporary Theatre Readings, and a mentorship from Lancaster University and the British Council. She wrote and performed *Original Skin* at the Market Theatre and the National Arts Festival in Grahamstown, and in 2006 won a Community Publishing Grant from the Centre for the Book to publish *Taller than Buildings*, which is now in its third edition.

de Villiers is a winner of the National Arts Festival/de Buren Writing beyond the Fringe Prize 2009 and received an Honourable Mention for her haiban 'Wanting' from the Kikakuza Haiban Society in Japan. She was was shortlisted for the Pen/Studinski Prize in South Africa.